ALL ıHINGS
AUTOMOBILIA

by Rob Arnold

All things Automobilia

ISBN: 978-1-910181-24-9

Published December 2015
First printed December 2015

Printed and Published by Anchorprint Group Limited

ARTICLES

WHERE DID IT ALL START?

I was born in the early fifties and spent my early years as an only child in a small village on the Leicestershire/ Derbyshire border.

The village was the base of a quarrying company and most folk in the village worked for them as drivers, quarry workers or in the workshops and offices. Not many back then owned cars in the village. I do remember the Vicar driving a Triumph Mayflower. However, my interest at an early age was watching the owner of the quarry, an ex military type, driving along in his magnificent Rolls Royce and some years later his son driving his car, a superb Aston Martin DB5. The Aston driver was the 'James Bond' of our village. With his Saville Row suits, suede shoes and hand made shirts he would park his Aston outside the offices, which just happened to be next to our village school. All the interested pupils would stand at the fence at lunchtime to see the Aston as the owner roared up the road on his way home for lunch, which incidentally was about eight hundred yards up the road. His father lived in the Hall situated in the middle of the village and I would often wait outside the massive gates to see his automobile glide through and up along the gravel drive. With it's huge tyres crunching as it glided along with no audible sounds from the silky smooth engine.

My first memories of motoring in our family, was the sight of my Grandfather's Hillman Imp arriving to collect my Mum and Dad and myself. It was usually to join my Grandparents on a rare outing, perhaps into the Peak District or a gentle Sunday drive out to Charnwood Forest.

It was a few years later that my Dad had his first vehicle, a Morris 1000 Van 9555 UE, with rear seats, totally immaculate and our ticket to freedom and a chance to explore. Dad later swapped the van for a 1959 MK1 Mini, 763 A0G.

At the age of twelve I purchased a 50cc motorbike with money I had earned from my paper round. Mum and Dad were not pleased but, as the bike was a non-runner, not a lot of concern was shown. I of course had other ideas and it was always my intention to get it running, which I did, and after school I would bomb around the local quarry.

This bike was the start of my motoring life and some fifty years later I am still involved with the trade. So how did I get into pumps and signs?

At the tender age of 15 I was thrust into the world of Automobilia as an apprentice in a small Derbyshire village garage. I will always have in my mind the sight of looking under benches in those first few weeks, and seeing an array of tools from a bygone age. It was immediately obvious that, in the past this garage started life as a blacksmiths shop, before going on to be a cycle repairers and eventually to motorcars. These tools comprised of all the hand tools, hammers, long shafted pliers etc. that you would find in the recreation of a blacksmiths shop at today's places such as The Black Country Museum and Beamish. To think that my association with motorcars goes back to those times and touched on that era is so far removed from an apprentice starting today, in a warm, well lit, floor painted dealership, with American tools gliding out of shiny red toolboxes. I never thought it could be so cold until that first winter. With part of the garage still being of wood construction, with ice on the inside of the windows and icicles hanging from the ceiling where part of the roof was leaking. We had a small coke burner in one corner that, for the first hour every morning, would putther out smoke, and the only realistic respite from the cold was to virtually sit right on top of it.

We had no fancy plastic, or mechanics, gloves that they use these days and having to run through to the small staff room to warm our hands under the hot tap at regular periods of the day. This caused our hands to become chapped and sore. Our feet didn't fare much better, even wearing three pairs of socks. On occasions you could literally feel the cold creeping through your bones and at the end of this long day, I had a cycle ride of several miles to get home to a warm bath and one of my mum's lovely hot dinners.

I was expected to do all the dirty jobs, from emptying grease soaked bins, to burning the rubbish out the back of the garage on a weekly basis. At the time I cycled to work, around four miles, from my home and on one occasion, after joining the business from school, I was so tired I fell off my bike and into a ditch and was happy to lie there until a mate pulled up in his van, having seen my bike plastered all over the hedge.

Those early days were tough and the only way to progress and work my way up was hard graft and a little planning. I soon realised that I had a knack of selling. I suppose I had what is called 'the gift of the gab'. But I also had honesty. People knew where they were with me; No clocking, ripping folks off or bodging up cars. If I was going to sell and deal with customers, I followed the rules laid down by my family. My Dad and both Grandads had high standards when it came to treating people in an honest and respectful manner.

I soon started to go out in the evenings and at weekends, selling cars for the dealership and for every car I sold I received a commission. Within a few short years I had worked myself up the ladder to become a director of the business. I was in charge of all the buying and selling. We rocketed up the league table of local dealerships and our sales went through the roof. It was at the time when British Leyland launched the Morris Marina and when I received my demonstration car for the showroom, I covered it in cloth and stoked up such local interest from the press that on the launch night the locals were banging on my office door to buy one.

I sold the first Marina to a then local celebrity, a man who had featured on TV for his farming knowledge. This triggered one of his Round Table mates to walk into my office demanding that the next Marina to arrive should have his name on it. At this time, this local businessman was driving around in a fabulous MK2 Jaguar, with leather seats, a wooden dash and quality that most would die for. I even pointed out that to trade in a Jaguar for a Marina needed careful thought and consideration. I also pointed out that the next four Marinas to arrive were all sold. This did nothing to quell the fire in his voice or his eyes; indeed, it seemed to enhance his desire to purchase a Marina. So much so that he then enquired what model the fifth Marina on our delivery sheet was. I told him that it was the top model and the price, at which point he took out his chequebook, wrote out a cheque for the full amount, and placed it on the table. A few weeks later the Jag was traded in against an 1800 four door Marina in Blaze Red with Mustard seats! The new price of the Marina was just over £1000, I gave him £50 for the Jag and I was happy at the time to trade it in for £55. Oh dear!

By the age of twenty I had become a director and taken the new car sales from around our ten a year to over one hundred. It was a British Leyland explosion around our way, with Minis, Morris 1000s, Oxfords and then of course the good old Morris Marina. It was boom time for the locals as cars were now available to the masses and I made sure the masses came to me. I was selling Marinas, Allegros and the like with mud flaps, sun roofs, vinyl roofs, Zebart and all these extras were covered by them taking out HP. Many were buying a new car for the first time. I sold to Quarry workers, local businesses and just about anyone who dared to walk into the showroom. I was on fire, I was racing Formula Ford and being sponsored by British Leyland to keep me sweet because I was selling plenty of their cars.

The next forty-five years were spent being connected with the garage trade in some form or another. I was asked by the Nat West Bank to help in a consulting role, helping them with a project in Burton on Trent, to turn around an ailing business which they had over stretched with loans. I went in and turned it around and found working in Burton was quite pleasant. I went on to own an MOT, service and car sales garage, supported by work from local businesses.

At the age of twenty my mode of transport was a Daimler Sovereign XJ6. This was at a time when most in our village were driving Morris 1000s, Vauxhall Vivas and Ford Cortinas. I was gliding along in sheer bliss.

It was never my intention to make others jealous or to give the impression of success. It was a genuine desire to own and drive quality, to be cocooned in a bubble of luxury, with the smell of leather, with that feel good factor only achieved by hard work and a need to reward oneself with the things in life that put a smile on your face.

I remember taking my XJ6 for a drive one winter's night on a deserted M1, from Markfield in Leicestershire to the North of Nottingham. I was alone and there was no one around, just a handful of cars and certainly in those days no police car to match my power. Having owned the car for just a few days I had yet to open her up, as they say. I approached the island at Markfield and joined the slip road to the motorway, pressing my right foot to the boards. The Daimler leapt into life like an exocet missile. Remember the cars of the day in our workshop were minis, Morris 1100's and Oxfords. The Daimler accelerated at a rate that I had not experienced before, pushing me hard into my seat and giving the impression that at the top of this incline, she was going to take off. As I joined the main carriageway I was literally launched into a world of Automobilia that remains the same within me some 40 plus years on.

FUEL FOR THOUGHT

It's hard to believe that the early motorist of the 20th century had to collect fuel from the local shop, be it the chemist, ironmonger or blacksmith.

Fuel would be delivered by rail to local railway stations, packed 2-gallon tins to a box. These were then delivered to the shops on handcarts or by horse and cart, direct from the refineries.

Motorists of the day were wealthy landowners or business men who had the necessary funds to allow them to be involved in the early days of motoring, seen by many at the time as a fad which would not last.

Empty two-gallon cans were then taken back to the shops to be returned to the refinery. There they would be cleaned, checked and reused many times.

As time progressed and motorists sought to venture further afield, a need to refuel during a journey soon became apparent. Often cans were strapped to the running boards, but a safer and more reliable source was required.

With the explosion of interest and the growth in this so-called fad, shops soon realised that with the quantities of fuel required, and the fact that cellars used to store fuel were not adequate, another method was needed.

Retailers looked to America, where isolated farms were using tanks and hand pumps on their premises. Soon several hand pumps were being used to transfer fuel from holding tanks. These pumps were the beginning of fuel delivery that, in so many ways, has not changed to the present day.

Fuel was delivered direct from the refinery in bulk and transferred to holding tanks, to be sold on to passing motorists.

It was not long before entrepreneurs could see an opportunity in the market and dedicated fuel stations were built at the side of roads, the first being in 1919 when the Automobile Association built it's first filling station at Aldermaston, which was manned by AA patrols. The birth of petrol stations came as oil companies saw the commercial possibilities and followed the AA's lead. Competition in the sale of fuel gave rise to a price war - in 1922 fuel cost 2 shillings per gallon, but by 1928 it had fallen to 1s 01/2d.

A price war was now underway and companies looked at advertising and presentation. Service stations were popping up everywhere and, to attract the passing motorist, they made the pumps bigger with globes to light up the pumps to attract the customer.

It was a nightmare for local councils who failed to keep up with the vast increase of properties selling fuel and, in some cases erecting no less than ten petrol pumps, all adorned with glass globes and massive signs advertising their product. Councils eventually realised that legislation was required to save every high street and village green being turned into a Las Vegas of lights and advertising.

Attendants were employed to crank these pumps to fill up the tanks of motorists but, as demand increased, a quicker and more efficient way was required and the introduction of electric pumps speeded up delivery and also prevented attendants from winning all the arm wrestling competitions in the pub!

For many years hand cranked pumps were retained as back up at many small retailers as these new electric pumps were not the most reliable and during power cuts, the old pumps were still required. Pumps were being produced in their thousands and most companies were building them under licence in several countries.

It is hard to believe that a hundred years later, not only do many of these pumps surface, mainly because of the quality of their construction, but also that they are now sought after as display items. If you own a single vehicle or a collection of vintage cars, there is no doubt that your display is enhanced by a vintage pump or a decorative sign.

I often use the phrase 'dress the scene' and on TV and film sets we are asked to do just that with our items, to add reality and nostalgia to a scene. On a regular basis we purchase pumps that are over a hundred years old and on stripping, in preparation prior to rebuild, we find that screws and bolts are removed with little effort, reflecting the quality and workmanship that went into producing these fantastic pumps.

We supply these pumps to decorate restaurants, pubs, games rooms and, of course, garages housing collections of vintage and classic cars. Wherever they are sited, the humble pump brings life and nostalgia to the scene.

GLASS GLOBES

In the boom years of early motoring, fuel companies went to great lengths to advertise and promote their goods. Villages and towns in the twenties were not known for glamour and glitz. These were places where you would find suited men with flat caps and ladies wearing anything but bright coloured clothing, where chimneys puffed out smoke and folk got their hands dirty. However, this was the age of the automobile, the new fad, as it was known. At the time someone said 'It would never take off'. The better off or middle to upper class had other ideas. Factory bosses, bank managers, solicitors and the like wanted to join the gentry in owning and running automobiles. After all their good wives were now wearing brightly coloured clothes and moving to the sounds of the Charleston, frequenting clubs and parties where the roaring twenties were well and truly swinging. They wanted to arrive at such venues in a motor-car and picnic beside the Thames, at places like Henley, on summer nights and weekends. This was a boom time for the car-makers and petrol companies and it was their job to attract such folk to buy their goods.

Dedicated petrol stations were shooting up all over the country. The first purpose built petrol station appeared in 1914 and by 1938 we had over 100,000. They were all competing with not only eye-catching livery and bright lights, but also a full-on price war at the pumps was taking place in the early twenties.

In 1922 petrol was 2 shillings a gallon but by 1928 it had halved to 1 shilling. Companies soon realised that, with competition, not only pricing but also a visual pull was needed. This is when pumps got bigger; globes were mounted on the top and illuminated to draw in the passing trade. Such a boom took place with some garages displaying up to ten pumps, all with globes and signs that lit up the grey skies over many towns. Councils were battling to control this new trend. BP alone had increased its petrol stations from a couple of hundred to 6,000 in a four year period in the twenties.

These globes that topped the pumps were just the 'icing on the cake', blown in moulds to take the shape of the company logo or just made bigger to stand out. They were all a sight to behold for the motorists of the time. We think of bright lights these days of, perhaps Oxford Street, Times Square or Las Vegas. In the twenties, when the average house had candle-light or the flickering light from a gas mantle, the local petrol station was their Las Vegas, with neon signs and globes lighting up the dim streets.

Almost 100 years on these glass globes that have survived the blitz and the test of time are highly collectable. Most were broken on removal, others just thrown away as time moved on. In the 1960's you could buy a shell fat body glass globe for a couple of pounds. By the 1990's you would be paying perhaps twenty or thirty. Today prices vary but £500 to £1,000 is not unrealistic. With globes taking up very little space, when illuminated we are transported back to those days of early motoring, to the sounds of the Charleston and visions of ladies with basin hats and feathers.

Go on buy yourself a globe!!

REPRODUCTION SIGNS AND GLOBES

Collecting classic and vintage cars is seen by many enthusiasts as something they do not have the funds to do, but you do not have to own a classic car or vintage automobile to be an enthusiast. In fact some collectors do so for investment purposes rather than for the love of collecting or automobilia.

We should all recognise that many who are not blessed with the means to indulge in ownership of top marques and expensive items have a right to enjoy nostalgia in ways that can be obtained by the limited funds available at the time. I recently had one guy in the showroom who thought it was quite wrong of me to stock reproduction signs and globes: an easy opinion if your wallet is laden with cash, but not everyone is so fortunate. We don't all shop at Marks & Spencer or Harrods but surely we all have a right to explore our nostalgic imagination and to fuel our desire to collect items we associate with our past. We don't all have the funds to buy and maintain a Ferrari or Rolls Royce but many happy hours are spent restoring and caring for the cheaper cars available for those who need a fix of yesteryear and memories of childhood.

We have signs in our showroom that sell for well over a thousand pounds and at an auction not so long ago a sign sold for ten times that amount. I am sure the purchaser gets satisfaction viewing the item in his display, but we also sell signs for under £100 and the folks who purchase them get equal satisfaction from the items they have purchased. At Automobilia we can decorate a 4 x 3 metre wall at a cost of over £10,000, but we could also decorate that same wall for £250 using reproduction items, and in both cases it would look stunning. And you know what? - Your neighbour or your friend would possibly not know the difference in value.

The Rolls Royce, Ferrari, Bentley, Morris Minor, Triumph Herald and 2CV all have a place and part to play in the world of automobilia and so does the bloke with the small budget. At Automobilia-UK we treat all customers with the same respect, whether they own a run of the mill 60's or 70's budget classic or a Ferrari super car.

Some years ago I owned a Rolls Royce Shadow 2 and a Morris 1000, both immaculate. Whilst out in the Rolls Royce, fellow drivers never gave way and indeed would take great pleasure in cutting me up, but in the Minor, drivers would wave you out, pip their horns and smile at you. I owned both cars for the pleasure I was getting driving them, certainly not for any showmanship. I was the same bloke behind the wheel of both cars but people judged me differently. We should not be so quick to judge those less fortunate with the funds that they have to pursue their interests in all things automobilia. We should welcome all to our world of automobilia and that includes reproductions as they all have a place and a part to play.

Cotswolds Garage

Cotswolds Garage

Showroom

Showroom

Showroom

Showroom

Showroom

Showroom

GADGETS AND SPECIAL EDITIONS

When travelling around the UK to classic car events and exhibitions, you very often come across stalls that have items produced using parts from the world of automobilia. This includes coffee tables made from F1 wheels, table lamps made from a crankshaft or sculptures crafted from nuts and bolts.

Some classic car enthusiasts fail to see the artistic value in such items and tend to think that the items used should not be removed from their original use. My opinion is, if such an item has been deemed unfit for its original use, then to give this item new life for it to remain in our world of automobilia can only be a positive step. After all, what would we do with redundant parts other than melt them down after they had become unfit for purpose.

I feel that it is important that these items of artwork are given value and certainly have a place in promoting interest in automobilia. In our workshop we create solid oak bases that are wired to light up and display our large glass globes and our small oil globes. We have sold these oak bases as single items for Christmas presents for people looking for that special gift to give to a classic or vintage car collector. On several occasions this has ignited the interest of the classic or vintage car enthusiast into branching out into the automobilia-collecting world.

From a single globe and base others have gone on to collect a full set of globes and when shown to friends and fellow enthusiasts, has sparked an interest further afield. The old saying goes 'from little acorns oak trees grow', a phrase I have used many times before. But in my mind, any artwork or sculpture that can trigger the need to collect in any individual can only be a positive outcome.

All profits from this publication will go to charity
with a set amount from each sale going to the
East Midlands Air Ambulance.

HOME RESTORATION
DOES IT PAY?

In garages and lock-ups around the UK classic cars, vintage cars and indeed vintage petrol pumps are sitting awaiting restoration by their once enthusiastic owners.

These items are often purchased at auctions or the small adds, and often seen as either an interesting project or a way of saving money by 'doing it ones self'.

Very often a start is made where, the would be restorer starts to strip down the said item. Only to find that perhaps work, family, or indeed health gets in the way and, by doing so making a start often reduces the value. In many cases the items are eventually sold at less than the original purchase price.

With my experience over the years, and also people I have met, has given me an insight into such goings on. Make no mistake, to restore an item, be it a car or a petrol pump, and to see the finished item in all it's splendour sitting in the garage. Gives a warm and satisfying glow to any restorer's face. That feeling of a job well done and that sense of pride as you show off the finished item to family and friends. A feeling you cannot achieve by just going out and buying it.

On the flip side, the disappointment and frustration you get opening the doors and seeing your project in pieces on a monthly basis. Or indeed yearly basis. Awaiting your attention and time is heart rending.

So many are drawn into the romantic notion of seeing an item brought back to life, without realising the work, finance and dedication involved.

If you have the time, finance, tools, workshop and skills to carry out a restoration then there is no better way to go.

If you think you are going to make a quick buck or that the job will be easy, then I would think again.

Cost wise, in my experience, it is often cheaper to buy a restored item than to spend the time and money on doing it yourself.

One of the best examples of this is the pedal car, Austin J40. The cost of new chrome, upholstery, tyres and paint, works out more than most restored cars are selling for. So buyers often find themselves out of pocket once they have purchased the 'restoration project' on internet sites.

My main advice to anyone buying a restoration project is not to start it until you have the time and funds, and to also carry out a thorough inspection of your item. With a costing of the items required to finish the job.

It may look a bargain at the time of purchase, but often these so called bargains become a white elephant and a financial headache.

AUTOMOBILIA

I am often asked who buys automobilia. Who would want a vintage petrol pump and what would they do with it. It is being recognised that automobilia is the 'new antique' and collectors come from all walks of life. At Automobilia-UK we have sold pumps to pensioners, TV stars, window cleaners, solicitors, teenagers and even delivered one to a knight of the realm on a private island.

These items are seen as a way of connecting to a motoring past that was only previously seen in photographs and news clips. Some of our clients have their pumps illuminated in studies, conservatories, offices and reception areas where they, along with their family, friends and clients take great satisfaction in reminiscing of a bygone age of motoring.

We supplied a pump to an insurance broker who, by his own admission, was not into automobilia, but had been advised by a colleague to install one in his reception as a feature and an icebreaker for his many classic car clients. Two weeks after we installed the pump he rang us to say that it was the best sales prop he had ever known, and clients loved to chat about the pump before they passed across their credit card to purchase an insurance policy.

One client purchased two pumps but warned us that, when we arrived to install them inside his house, his wife could possibly, as he put it 'kick-off', as he had not told her of his recent purchase. She had given him so much grief regarding unfinished car restorations on the drive. The delivery day arrived and we pulled up outside the house. Luckily his wife was at the hairdressers, so we quickly installed the pumps and I told my colleague to start up the van so that we could escape before she returned. I plugged both pumps into the electric sockets and flooded the house with light and sheer nostalgia. As we stood back to admire these wonderful 1950's icons the client turned to me and said, "If she doesn't like them she will have to go". He wasn't talking about either pump! Just as he finished speaking the door flew open - his wife had arrived back home to see a van outside with the words 'Automobilia-UK' all over the sides and she feared the worst. Another old wing, a pair of bumpers or perhaps even another old car but, as she entered the room she looked straight past us and at these statue-like, shiny, bright and indeed wonderful display items. We all took a gulp of air and she spun around and hugged her better half. She thought they were, as she put it, 'stunning'. After which she put the kettle on and out came the chocolate digestives. She then, in no uncertain terms, told her husband to now cash in some of the cars he would never finish, clear the garage and buy more of these beautiful pumps. They now own seven at the last count and both are very happy.

Of course they have also moved on to signs etc. to dress the scene and are now very much into automobilia.

'Better than money in the bank'.

FROM THE VICARAGE TO AMERICA

For many years in my early days, I used to look after a Vicar's car who lived in the village not far from where we lived. I would collect his car and carry out repairs and maintenance as required. He was never the jolly friendly type who would make you feel welcome or ask you in for a cuppa. He was quite stern and had the personality of a seasoned headmaster, rather than a people loving man of the cloth. He would quiz me on what had been done to his car in detail but not in a warm or inquisitive way, but in a way that made me feel a little uncomfortable. Of course he had every right to enquire what work had been done, but I would have gladly given him details had he given me the chance to chat over a cuppa. But his way was straight to the point and he expected details in full. On the return of his vehicle and the said interrogation, he would never pay on the day. It was almost as if he needed to try the goods before purchase. I would have to return for payment a couple of weeks later where, again I would be asked to give details of repairs before his cheque book was taken from his hall drawer and, once filled out, would be thrust at me and the door would be opened for me to make my exit. And so the experience was never a pleasant one. He refused to deal with anyone else at the garage and, should I be on holiday for instance, he would wait for my return rather than deal with any of the others. Often my relatives who attended his Church would tell me how he would ask of my well being and heap praise on how I looked after him and what a 'smashing', as he would tell them, lad I was. I used to think that's all well and good and nice to hear, but goodness knows what his treatment of me would have been had he not liked me. Having said all this I had a schoolmaster at primary and a form teacher at secondary school who were stern and strict, but I had the utmost respect for them and for all their sharpness and perhaps cold approach. I respected the Vicar in the same way and I was never going to be anything but kind to him as I was to all of our customers.

One year, at MOT time for his car, it became very obvious that the car the Vicar was using to visit his flock had seen better days, and that the time was ripe for him to replace his vehicle. I was now faced with the prospect of explaining this to him and, going on past experience, this would be no easy task. I arrived at the Vicarage, knocked on the door and was summoned in by a loud, "The door is unlocked". I turned the large cast knob on the door and entered. I felt like I was being thrown to the lions. I entered the large, cold, high ceilinged entrance and stood there until I was instructed to "come through", into the large Victorian kitchen where the Vicar sat eating his meal. "Come in, come in", he bellowed and as he continued to eat his meal I explained the state of his car. At no point was I invited to sit and seldom did he lift his head as he listened to my analysis. My voice must have resembled a child being asked to explain how he had broken a window with his football. I could feel my mouth drying up and the words starting to stutter. Once I had given my report, there was a long pause before he raised his head and he gave his response. He proceeded to tell me that he needed a car to tend his flock and that it was now my job to find him one and sooner rather than later. At that point my pathetic child like 'Oliver to Fagin' voice again appeared. "Yes Sir", I will Sir, straight away Sir". At which he bellowed. "Well go on then boy, go and find me a car". I was then shown the door. I have to add here that I was not a boy. I had recently bought a house and was married but, to him, I was a 'boy'. My heart sank as I drove away, at the prospect of finding a car that would, not only be up to scratch for this fussy individual, but the time it would take to persuade him to part with his money.

As luck had it, my father in law was looking for a smaller car to replace his Austin Cambridge; perhaps this would fit the bill. The Austin was in excellent condition and was a car I knew inside and out and so I found my father in law a smaller car and offered the Austin to the Vicar. To my amazement he loved it. On a test drive he sped through the lanes around the village and was happy with my choice for him. I then went on to explain that the car came with, as he could see, a very nice registration number, 3 BRC. I explained that I wanted to retain ownership of this and asked if he would agree to me buying back the car once he had finished with it in the years to come. He agreed, especially as I reduced the price for this agreement. Nothing was written down in agreement to this, after all he was a Vicar.

I looked after the car for him over the next few years, until one day I was informed that he had sadly passed away. Almost three months passed and by now I had given up hope of ever getting the Austin and, indeed the number plate back. At the time the value of the plate would have been around fifty to one hundred pounds. Then, out of the blue, I was visited at the garage by an official looking, smart gentleman in a suit. He explained that his father had passed away and left me a car in his will. It was to my surprise the Vicar's son. I had no idea that he had a son but was told that his father thought a great deal of me and that he wanted to thank me personally for looking after his father regarding his vehicles.

I was asked to sign a document accepting this bequest and I was pleased to do so as I thought I was getting my registration number back. On signing I admit that a lump came to my throat as I remembered the old boy, who spoke so well of me and, having passed away, had not forgotten me. Having signed the said document a set of keys was handed to me along with all the documents to the car, at which point I noticed the keys were not those of the Austin, but I was now the new owner of the Vicar's pride and joy: his Jaguar MK 7 saloon!

I was unaware that the Vicar owned such a car and had no recollection of ever seeing it. I was then asked if I could remove the Jag from its garage as soon as possible, to which I agreed. The following day I collected this MK 7 Jag which, despite having been in storage for quite some time, started first time and I drove it back to the garage. I had nowhere to store it, it was far too big for me to dash in and around and I certainly had little time to give to it with a new house and blushing new bride.

A few days later I was informed by one of the staff that a man was looking at the Jag. I went out to see him and we got chatting about the car and how I had come by it. He was a part time driver/car restorer from Leicester. He made me an offer and a deal was done, with me receiving a great deal more than what the number plate was worth. I became good friends with the buyer and watched the Jag's progress as he restored it. Eventually he sold it to a contact in America. I never did see the Austin again and, of course, never owned 3 BRC but somewhere out there is that number plate and, somewhere up there is a Vicar who thought enough of me to leave me a bequest that funded a few projects around our newly purchased home.

WHAT A COLLECTION

A few years ago I spotted a pedal car in an auction, well when I say pedal car it was actually a pedal plane.

The auctioneer explained to me that a wealthy family had commissioned the plane to be built for young family members at quite an expense. The plane was wooden and fitted with bespoke items to compliment its bespoke build.

With a wingspan of around five feet and a similar size in length, this was quite a stunning item and, although I had no real call to buy it, I certainly had an interest in it.

I left an offer with the auction house and after a couple of days I was the proud owner.

I advertised the plane on the internet and received a call from a lovely chap in Worcestershire enquiring about the item. A deal was struck over the telephone and I was to deliver the following week.

On the day of delivery my wife was on her day off work, so she came along for the ride. When we arrived at the property, electric gates allowed us to enter the gravelled drive, which then opened up onto a gravelled parking area. The views of a beautiful detached property, surrounded by paddocks and lawned areas greeted us.

The patio had a large Koi Carp pond with wrought iron table and chairs and several ornamental statues. It was a lovely day and I was showing the elderly gentleman the plane, which was in the back of my van. His wife came out and invited my wife for a coffee on the beautiful patio. When the customer and myself joined them they were deep into conversation about holidays and in particular the QE2, which they had spent so many happy times aboard, just as we also had done.

The next hour was spent reminiscing about our experiences afloat and we were getting along fine. Then his wife looked across and asked her husband if he was going to show me his collection. After a pause in thought he said that he would.

At this point I was informed that only family had ever been invited to see the items concerned and that even his postman of twelve years, who had delivered so many items by post, and was curious to view his collection, had not been allowed.

By this time I was intrigued but certainly not prepared for the sight that was to be put before me.

Looking across the lawn, I had spotted a very large building which looked like a WW2 type, covered in a black tar covering like those found on military aerodromes to store items.

It was dark and unassuming on the outside but what lurked inside was an explosion of automobilia, colour, smell and sheer nostalgia.

This was one man's private collection of pumps, globes, signs, pedal cars, Dinky and Corgi cars, uniforms and all other items connected to automobilia.

Everything was displayed in 'museum like' tidiness and everything had its place. Oak cabinets were full of motoring items such as driving gloves, Chauffeurs hats, AA and RAC memorabilia and vintage lamps.

Both my wife and myself stood in disbelief at the sight of such a fantastic collection. For the next two hours we inspected the rooms, which housed the many different items on show.

This collection had been put together over many years for the sole pleasure of the collector, but I have no doubt that so many would be blown away by this place, had they been given the chance to see it.

I would estimate that the number of items housed there would be in excess of two thousand, possibly more.

I have never seen so many Corgi and Dinky models in one collection, and a row of over twenty pedal cars in mint condition. Several fully restored pumps; globes and signs also took pride of place.

A collection of cycles, many hanging from the beams,were along with the by-planes, and items of motoring past.

Drawers were full of car badges, brochures, books and stickers.

At one end of the main building were vintage cars, cloaked in protective covers, which were removed to delight us with the sight of motoring glory days.

This was a private gentleman with a fantastic private collection, who had no plans to share his items with the outside world. We felt privileged and very lucky to have been invited to view his collection that rivals any I have seen to date.

FROM LITTLE ACORNS

We were recently commissioned by one of our clients to design the interior of his classic car garage. Measuring almost 70' x 35', this was not a matter of just filling it with vintage pumps and signage. In fact the customer had requested that the floor area was to be kept clear to aid the storage of his exotic collection.

With this in mind it was apparent that we needed imaginative ideas to bring this huge area alive, without just plastering walls with large signs.

We quickly decided to design and create murals depicting decades of motoring. One of these murals would be of a 1920's motorcar backing into a workshop, undergoing repairs. At the front of the scene our idea was to position a period trolley jack. Being of this period these jacks were only approximately 6" wide and in being so would not encroach too much onto the valuable floor space.

Although we had one of these jacks in stock, we decided to look for another specimen, as the one we had was often hired to TV and film companies to dress scenes. A few days later we spotted one for sale on an internet site that was little more than half an hour away from our showroom. I quickly rang the seller, agreed a price and also enquired if he had any other automobilia items.

At that point he began to list what he had in stock and I quickly realised that this was not a case of sending someone to collect the item - this was a collection and visit that I had to do myself.

If you talk to dealers of antiques and collectables, they will often joke about an instinct they have to source items and to establish a bond with useful contacts. This was one of these occasions. My instinct told me that I needed to meet this particular seller who, on the telephone sounded quite mature and knowledgeable of the items he possessed.

When I arrived at what was a modest semi-detached house in a small town some 20 miles from our showroom, a young man, perhaps in his late 20's, greeted me He quickly offered his hand as he explained that he knew who I was and that for some time had been following our website and my exploits. I was still not sure if this was the guy I had spoken to on the phone or if indeed he would lead me around the back to meet his father perhaps.

It was, however, quickly established that he indeed was the person I had spoken to earlier that day. With pride and obvious passion he led me through a side door, passing fences and walls adorned with advertising signs, and we approached what can only be described as a modest garden shed, little more than 10' x 8'. As he opened the door to reveal the contents, I was immediately struck by the sheer volume of items and also by the neat and organised fashion that the contents were displayed in.

As the conversation flowed the excitement quickly gathered pace, not by the vision of contents in front of me, but my overwhelming delight at finding a young man who was just setting out on his journey of discovery and interest, in a world that existed many decades before he was born.

It is so easy for people of my generation to get involved and show interest in items that they remember with fondness from childhood. Such items as Scalextric, early mobiles, computer games and daytime TV would have surrounded this young man at an early age. It is therefore more remarkable and refreshing to find this young man surrounded by items from the past, items that would have been recognised more by his parents or grandparents. Everywhere that I looked in this small shed, items were neatly placed and organised, many of them labelled with a short description and approximate year of manufacture. Items such as 1950's/60's shabby chic suitcases, oil bottles, cans and jugs, signs and shop display items including original bars of soap from this era.

As the conversation continued we spoke of his passion, and quickly established that he had a market for certain items that we often obtain through buying complete collections or stock through our business, that we could put his way.

This was not a case of taking this young man under my wing. This level headed young man was doing more than ok with the knowledge he had and his obvious skill in spotting a bargain and items that others would find interesting. I also realised that this was an opportunity for our business to have another pair of sharp eyes, scouring the market place for items we could use for TV and film hire.

I was so impressed by this young man; his attitude and knowledge, his organisation and above all his passion, that I feel it is our duty and indeed will be our pleasure to encourage him in the future.

From little acorns oak trees grow.

*The family
at BBC
Nottingham
studios*

*On board
Queen Elizabeth
with RL sales
girls*

A night on board QM2

A trip to Ireland to deliver pumps

We sponsor a school football team

Alan T and Alan S photographed with players on the day we sponsored a match

My good friends at Mathewsons

With Gari and our mutual friend Toni, outside his coffee shop Casuso, Derby

BAFTA screening in Cardiff with Director Rob Sanders

Me with customer and good friend Steve

Meet and greet on Salvage Hunter as cameras roll

Good day filming with Drew and Tee

*James Martin
and Rob Arnold*

James Martin with me at LCCS

*James Martin with our props at the
London Classic Car Show Launch*

James Martin with our props

*Alan and Richard
at the showroom*

Wheelers Dealers Mike and Ed at a press day

Town crier in Liverpool tells everyone to visit our site! loudly!

Ex F1 chief mechanic Robin Baxter visits showroom

Gari Glaysher signs up for garage opening performance

ALL THINGS AUTOMOBILIA

Summer Holiday

Last minute notes before talk on Queen Mary 2

My Formula Ford days

Me with the Caddy used in the film Pink Cadillac driven by Clint Eastwood

My Cotswolds garage creation

LCCS press launch

Signing up to Rareburg TV in London

Sons take over on stand at LCCS

Our stand at London car show 2015

Our graphic man Derek at DG printers Measham

ROME WASN'T BUILT IN A DAY

Two years ago I was contacted by a client regarding an item for sale on our website, nothing unusual about that you might think, but as we chatted away I became more and more intrigued at what he was telling me about his collection or, more to the point, the building housing his collection, and the work required to build it. It was one of those phone calls where you know a visit is required to satisfy your curiosity.

This guy lived on the outskirts of Sheffield and I quickly agreed to deliver the items he had just purchased on my way up North the following week. As many will know Sheffield is built on and around hills - like Rome but without the gladiators and the sun. Most roads in and around the city and surrounding area are indeed on a hill and as I pulled up outside his house it too was on a steep incline. Looking at the house from the road this neat and tidy residence had a homely look about it that was well kept and in first class repair with a large front porch and plenty of windows flooding the reception area with lots of light. To one side was the neighbouring property and to the other an up and over garage door with parking to the front for two cars and, adjoining the garage, the start of the other neighbour's house. So immediately it was apparent that no vehicle access to the rear of the property was obtained from the front.

As I approached the house the garage door opened and for the first time I met and shook hands with the owner who led me into the single garage. Leading from the garage through a door at the rear was a well stocked and neatly set out workshop with tools arranged and mounted on display boards. The floor and walls were immaculate with several decorative signs and vintage items strategically placed to enhance the décor. What was more than evident at this point was the fact that this guy was not only meticulous in his neatness and organisation but he was heavily into motorbikes! Leading out from this den of a workshop we entered a small courtyard and the first sight of what can only be described as a well-built brick faced building with reclaimed bricks and mortar which, you could tell, had been put together with love and dedication.

I was by now most impressed and, not only liking what was put in front of me, but warming to my host with every word he spoke. He then proceeded to open the door and I stepped into this amazing private museum of motorcycle and automobilia nostalgia. I must add at this point that I am not a motorcycle expert and know very little about things with two wheels and usually am not easily excited by vintage bikes. But outside, before I stepped through this door, I was informed by the owner that dozens of tons of earth had to be dug and transported through the garage to remove part of the banked garden to erect this building. This was, and is, be it small, a motorcycle museum built into a hillside not far from the city of Sheffield, that neighbours and locals would be amazed to find.

I have visited Rome on several occasions and I am always moved by the architecture and the effort and sacrifice made by those who created such a place. It would be foolish to compare the enormity of Rome with a small plot in Sheffield but if all those individuals working on the Pantheon and, the Colosseum had the same desire and work ethic of this chap, no wonder we have the spectacle we all enjoy and admire today.

 Having been told that he had built all this in remembrance of his late father, I have to admit a lump came into my throat and I felt quite moved. At which point I turned to shake this man's hand and immediately we hugged each other because he had realised that his story and hard work had touched me and I had so much respect for him. This was a man I had met only twenty minutes before. We were immediately united by the love of automobilia and the sheer effort and hard graft of its sensitive display. This guy worked hard to provide for his family and at the same time to build his dream of a motorcycle museum in memory of his late father.

The inside was decked out with shelving that was laden with items from a bygone age of motorcycling. Several motorbikes were neatly arranged beneath a worktop that ran the full length of the building on top of which were placed more motorcycles and memorabilia.

One of the motorbikes belonged to his late father and took pride of place. Every bike had a story and he took great pleasure in telling me the history, the work he had carried out and the hours of love he had put into them. At one end of the building was what looked like a guitar amp and, enquiring about this, he opened the door to reveal a fridge containing a collection of beers. At the other end stood a vintage petrol pump topped with a globe, giving off a shaft of light which danced off the glossy paint on the tanks of these superb motorcycles. This was in no way the most expensive or vast collection of automobilia that I had seen in private hands but this guy had not only removed a mass of soil and stone to give access to a plot, he had hand built the unit with a labour of love and restored most of the contents.

I travel the country looking at collections and I am blown away on many occasions at what I see. A garage full of Ferraris, a mansion with outbuildings large enough to house a rock concert but through no fault of their own some of these guys are born with a silver spoon. Most have never got grease on their hands or worried about bank balances. Oh, they are genuine collectors and we need these guys to put their money into our world of automobilia but they would be first in line to acknowledge that the sacrifices made and the hard work of this chap in Sheffield is something to congratulate and admire.

I have since sold this man, whom I now regard as a friend, several items including pumps, globes and signs. I have got to know his wonderful family and enjoy his company whenever I venture into the hills of Sheffield. This is also the man who paid me the ultimate compliment when he said that he had told his other half that, if anything should happen to him, she should contact me to help her dispose of his collection because he trusted me to look out for her. As a friend I am proud of what he has achieved. I am also proud of the fact that he thinks so much of me to suggest this to his other half.

I often tell people that I love my work; I am also lucky that I meet and befriend such wonderful people and all in the name of Automobilia.

All profits from this publication will go to charity
with a set amount from each sale going to the
East Midlands Air Ambulance.

DR WHO

I took a call one day from a guy who was interested in purchasing a petrol pump. As the conversation progressed, we realised that we had some common ground - not only our interest in automobilia, but also that many years ago we had both lived in the same town. As we both tossed names in the air from our past, we ascertained that our 'contact book' overlapped in many cases.

Although I remained in the same area, he was now living sixty miles south in the Cotswolds. As the conversation eventually got back to the business in hand, we quickly decided on a vintage pump and a deal was struck. He explained that building work was taking place at his property and his purpose built garage, to house his collection of classic cars, was far from being complete. He requested that we hold on to the pump until at least the heavy, dusty work to complete his project, had been carried out.

A couple of months later, he informed me that although the work was not yet complete on the garage, he was now in a position to take delivery. So a few days later the pump was loaded onto the van and I travelled down to the Cotswolds, to be confronted by an unbelievable set-up.

The sat nav took me to a small village, deep in the heart of the beautiful Cotswolds. This was not a part of the world where the majority of properties have a house number. This was a community where house names are your only point of contact. At this stage the only option was to telephone the client to ask for directions. We quickly agreed, after I have given him my location, that I was indeed pointing in the right direction. I was told to follow the lane until I came to two large pillars adorned with creatures from the wild. At the large electric gate I tapped in the security code which I had been given, the large oak gates then started to open, allowing me access to the long gravelled drive.

Travelling down the drive and glancing over to my left, I had my first view of the most beautiful Cotswold stone built hall. You would think at this point, having spoken to the client, and now having seen the property, I would be prepared for what I was about to see at this fabulous location. The gentleman in question was standing in a gravelled courtyard, with the house in the background, and what looked like a ten foot high wall that ran from the corner of the property, along the side of the courtyard that was reminiscent of walls found to protect kitchen gardens at National Trust type properties.

In the centre of this wall was a pair of oak doors that upon opening you could imagine being led into a garden or lawned area. What I was about to discover was that behind these doors was the home to his classic car collection. As I walked into the building, immediately in front of me was a large turntable sunken into the floor. This was to allow vehicles to be driven onto and then rotated, to enable easy manoeuvring into position.

Builders were still on site at this point and the project was far from being finished, but I would have no doubt that when the petrol pump was in situ, and the walls were adorned with signs and motoring artefacts, this would be the envy of most classic car enthusiasts.

Over in the corner I spotted a doorway, which led to a corridor, or might I say a tunnel, leading to the house. This was to give the owner easy access to his collection. Halfway along the tunnel a washroom, shower and toilet were being built. On the garage side of this door, in the corner, a tardis was being erected – a replica of the one used by Dr Who.

At this time, with building work still in progress, only a couple of the client's cars had found their new home, each covered in tailored jackets. On removal of these covers, both cars were prime examples of their marques.

I returned to the van and set off for my journey home. This gave me time to reflect on what I had seen that day. This was a man who had obviously done well in life, had a vision for what he wanted to achieve and had a passion for the things he collected and, furthermore, will hopefully be a valued customer in the future.

I had to chuckle at my vision of him perhaps greeting a visitor outside the wall. I could imagine him leading them from the kitchen and through the tunnel, reminiscent to those used in stately homes over a hundred years ago, allowing staff to move between house and garden without being seen from the windows in the main house. He would lead them past the washroom, through the tardis and into a haven of nostalgia. Should he decide to bring them in the other way, they would enter the wall, through the oak doors, be rotated 90° on the turntable and driven into a space. On exiting the vehicle, they would admire the contents around them, enter the tardis and be led along the tunnel and into the house.

How cool is that?

Eighteen months following the delivery of the petrol pump and on his return from the winter in Australia, this same client made an appointment to visit our showroom.

On viewing the items in stock and, following a tour of the premises, including the paint shop etc where out pumps are restored, we returned to my office for a mid-morning coffee. The client explained that he would like to commission us to completely dress his garage, with was over seventy foot long and well over thirty foot wide, with automobilia. He was offering me a blank canvas to use all of our skills to create something special in this unique setting.

As we sat there my mind raced with ideas and a vision of what we could create, from solid oak lamp display brackets, themed walls, a garage scene at one end and commissioned artwork depicting vintage scenes of motoring nostalgia. I think that it is fair to say that the ideas which I was creating on paper in front of him were no doubt exciting him and no doubt my enthusiasm was also ticking the boxes. We very quickly agreed a budget and more importantly a deal for Automobilia-UK to secure the photographic and filming rights on the day of the official opening. Contracts were quickly drawn and work began immediately.

One of the first tasks was to get all those involved in the project together in a meeting to discuss ideas and plans. This involved Alan the wood turner, Richard our restorer, Abbi our artist, Derek and Michelle from the graphics team and of course Alan T, my second in command. I explained the project to them and the importance of what this could mean to our business. It wasn't new to us to dress a complete garage and work with a client who would chose items themselves, but here we had a guy who was trusting us with a blank canvas and complete control of what items we used, with the end result being shown on videos on our website and on the TV channel Rareburg.com. Plus a worldwide audience on social network.

All of the team came up with ideas and were excited by the project. Although the opening day would be a private occasion, with a sprinkling of some very distinguished guests, I was well aware of the end result with photographs and TV footage being shown around the world. With this in mind I organised supercars such as a Ferrari, McLaren, Rolls Royce and a Manx Norton motorcycle, which on the day would be filmed entering the garage through a 'smoke haze' with lighting effects onto the turntable which would be rotated 360 degrees. All being played out as a live performance by a well know opera singer was taking place. This was after all a special location with a special client and this just had to be a very special day.

WELSH GOLD

At Automobilia-UK we receive emails or telephone calls on a daily basis from people wanting to sell automobilia, from single items to full collections. Some are rewarding for the potential profit, others are just interesting for the nostalgia value, and talking to the characters on the end of the telephone.

A couple of years ago I took a call from a gentleman who explained that he had recently retired and wanted to dispose of the items in his garage business, a business that he had shared with his brother for the past half century. Such a phone call initially gets the pulse racing, not from the profit potential, but for a glimpse maybe into a motoring world long gone, and hard to find in this modern age. I initially agreed to visit the premises and indulge myself hopefully into such a world.

On arrival I was not disappointed, and found a garage setting which could have been from the fifties or sixties - old wall charts, tin signs and an old Michelin mascot hanging from a beam, all of which were covered in dust and cobwebs, giving the word patina a new meaning. This part of the business had survived because in the early seventies a new building with MOT facilities had been erected across the yard and rendered the part that I was now in, almost redundant.

I was in mid Wales with the two brothers reminiscing about an age long gone but with memories of the garage trade that I could relate to as I had worked in a similar type of workshop as a young fourteen year old many years before. When one of the brothers opened the garage door to let in the sunlight, it was like looking at the start of a movie that was promising to transport the onlooker to a bygone world of nostalgia. As the light shone inside you almost expected an aged mechanic, with grease sodden boiler suit, flat cap and a cigarette drooping in the corner of his mouth, to step out and stretch his arms. Thankfully this did not happen. I stepped inside and, for what seemed like an age, I stood in complete silence, just gulping in the sheer nostalgia. A shaft of light was hitting the Michelin man hanging from that beam and I swear I saw him smile - and if I didn't then he should have done.

The smell, or should I say aroma, was straight from the fifties garage where the smell of thick axle grease, paraffin and carbon fuse together to give you that recipe for nostalgia. I breathed in slowly and then out again, like you would at the top of a Swiss mountain or a pine forest in Norway. My lungs were full of this special cocktail that is just impossible to replicate and even harder to explain to those who have never experienced it.

I was just soaking up the atmosphere when, after what seemed to be an age, I heard the two brothers chatting to me and asking if I was interested in this or that, but I was gone with the impact that this place was having on me. After a while I started to respond to their requests. They kept pointing at items and shouting out prices they requested and I just kept saying yes. Over five hours were spent going through boxes and cupboards giving light to items that had not been used for decades. In fact, even the brothers could not recall when some of the items were used or even last seen, but every item they did remember came with a story or some description of where it was purchased or whose car it was last used on. These veteran mechanics knew the prices and values of what they had, but were more interested in finding good homes for the items they had worked with for decades. Just before I was ready to depart I spotted a door on the back wall and enquiring what was behind it I was told that there would be nothing of interest in there for me, as this was a store for old oil filters and air filters. I accepted this but asked if I could have a quick look anyway. On opening the door I was faced with more cobwebs and dust and I did find a stack of filters, but lurking in doors and cupboards were old carded items that used to be found in petrol stations and garages in the 1950's and 60's. Such items as tape on card, packets of fuse wire on cards, fuses and bulbs. These were items that I could use for dressing film and TV sets, and to me were an excellent find. The brothers were so pleased that I was offering them money for items that they were just going to throw in a skip.

Finally I closed the door on the van, gave the two brothers a handshake and a hug and off I went back to base with the two elderly gentlemen happily waving me down the road.

NOW THAT'S WHAT I CALL A BARN FIND

Many times when people discover what I do for a living, they will inform me about a collection owned by a friend or family member, which they suggest I must see. It usually ends with them sending me an email with contact details of the person with the collection and perhaps a few photographs.

Over the years I have been fortunate to see some fantastic collections, many of which are private and unseen by outsiders. These can include Ferraris and the like, with values way into the millions. Because I have a reputation to maintain I think, in some cases, this gives celebrities and owners the confidence in knowing that I cannot discuss or disclose their location.

Our reputation is built around discretion and trust and our clients, of which we have 'titled' and 'A' list customers need us to maintain that confidence.

It is sometimes a little amusing when you visit such a collection one day worth millions to be shown around a collection the following day, perhaps only worth a few hundred pounds. But what is important to remember is the latter has the same value to the owner in terms of achievement, as the garage full of supercars, and in may cases appreciated more. With all this in mind it is sensible not to get too excited when a collection, that I must see, is mentioned and, to be honest, when a friend informed me of a collection of cars in a barn not too far from where I live and, especially as the barn was situated on a farm and it was explained that it was 'a bit of a mess' and untidy, no bells were ringing or pulse racing and certainly no sweaty palms. Indeed it was a further twelve months before I decided to ring the owner to arrange a visit.

On the day of the visit, I collected my friend and set off for the location, with him explaining that it had been a few years since his last visit and, from what he could remember there were several, as he put it 'old cars', which he could not recall makes or indeed exactly how many, but it would be an afternoon jaunt. And the owner would no doubt make us a cuppa.

We turned off the main road, down a farm track, passing several buildings and into the farmyard. The main house was not particularly attractive, not the usual rambling, three storey building reminiscent of farmhouses in this area. The yard was free of the stuff cows, and other livestock deposit, on the concrete outside outbuildings, so this was not what you associate with a working farm. A few cars that had seen better days, such as a Triumph TR7 and what looked like a Vauxhall Nova, were parked in an abandoned state at the far end of the yard covered in, what looked like a decade of grime. With ivy lapping over the roofs, so no excitement was bubbling inside at this point.

The owner then emerged from the house and with a firm, strong handshake, this ordinary, unassuming, pleasant man, invited us in for a cuppa. It was a typical farmhouse with wife in the kitchen, dog on his favourite seat, wellies placed on newspaper, a log burner in the corner and comfy chairs with loose covers only removed on Chapel days.

I sat there listening to tales from bygone days between my friend, who had recently retired, and the farmer who was in his seventies.

At no point was I aching to escape the banter and view the buildings, I was warm, the logs were giving off a rosy glow, the second cuppa had arrived and the dog was still fast asleep. Plus the outside temperature was only just above freezing. So, it was with some reluctance, that when our host rose to his feet and invited us to view his 'old bangers' as he put it, that I thought of suggesting another cuppa and perhaps view another day, But by now he had slipped his wellies on and was halfway out the door with my friend in tow and the dog following on.

We entered the yard and then waited in the cold while several locks were opened and alarms were switched off and the huge barn door slid open. Lights were then triggered and as the fluorescent lights flickered into life the most unbelievable sight met my eyes and lit up my face.

I was rooted to the spot, having stepped into this amazing theatre of dreams. Before me was a sea of E Types, T R's and Morgans. This was no ordinary character of a man and this was no ordinary barn find. For the next hour plus, I wandered through an array of cars, parts and outbuildings filled with the kind of items that send a shiver down an enthusiast's spine.

On one four post lift was a flat bottom E Type, in the corner was a Morgan Three Wheeler and under a bench I could just make out the front of a T R 3.

As I wandered through this wonderland more cars were emerging, including several more E-Types, another Morgan, a couple of XJ8's, a Triumph Roadster and many more.

Tools littered the floor; cobwebs danced in the breeze as I hurriedly went past them in my pursuit of more excitement of the riches before me. Jaguar engines, T R gearboxes, boxes of valuable parts and several E Type bonnets were there to be seen.

Moving on to another barn I found vintage motorbikes, half hidden by even more items that had been accumulated by this somewhat eccentric collector. In another store on the opposite side of the yard, I literally had to move boxes of items to see what was housed in the adjoining rooms and, to my amazement, I found the contents of what could only have been a complete cycle shop. Hanging from the beams were several lengths of rope supporting dozens of cycle wheels. When I later enquired how the owner had obtained all this cycle equipment he explained that a few years ago he was offered the contents of a cycle shop, which was closing down.

This was not just an ordinary collector, this was a guy who when offered goods he was interested in he did not have the ability to just say no.

Seeing all the other items around his property, this must have been the case on many occasions.

During the afternoon I tried in vain several times to purchase items but with no joy. People such as these can be referred to as collectors or indeed hoarders but in my experience to them money is not the value; they just have a reluctance to let anything go.

I have returned several times since and the owner has agreed for me to photograph the collection for a future book and, of course, the location and the owner's identity will be respectfully protected.

The photographs here are just to give you an idea of the items that abound at this location.

I recently paid another visit but I hasten to add, not to buy but to deliver items, which he had asked me to find for him.

All this and a stones throw from my front door you never know what is around the corner or behind those closed doors !

Collectors and collections come in many forms !!!!!

Filming in Penzance for Channel Four

My debut on TV show

Salvage Hunter

In front of camera for History Channel

Filming for Salvage Hunter

Filming for Rareburg TV

Turbo pickers TV show

On set for feature film with actors

ALL THINGS AUTOMOBILIA

Our pump on film set in 2014

One of our pumps delivered

Our van on set

We visit the set of Heartbeat

Lights camera action

Our pump and props in Ralph Lauren London store

Our pumps on ITV sponsors set for Jekyll and Hyde

Our pump with Bentley

*Our pumps in background
on BBC one show 2014*

Clients collection in the north of England

New van from Ford UK

Bergerac Triumph was on our site for sale

ITV commercial add with our pumps

Jaguar XJ6 my first taste of luxury motoring

Our base at Burton on Trent

My Mum and Dad inspect new showroom

Motor Cycle collection - Rome was not built in a day

Motor Cycle collection in Sheffield

MC collection Sheffield

Barn find

Barn find

Barn find

RIGHT PLACE RIGHT TIME

Some time ago I was on a delivery in North Yorkshire when I took a call from a guy in Leeds, asking if I could call and give him some advice on some vintage signs in his late father's garage. He went on to explain that his father was a classic car enthusiast, a pastime and passion he sadly did not share with him. His mother had asked her son to clear dad's garage as she was selling the property to downsize to a more manageable dwelling. When the guy informed me that he was in Leeds, I explained that I was on my way back from a trip in Yorkshire and, if he was agreeable, I could be at the property within the hour. He agreed and the sat nav destination was punched in.

On my arrival I was greeted by the guy and led to a wonderful garage/workshop, which had been his late fathers workshop, den and pleasure palace for the past four decades. There was a four-poster ramp at one end with a vintage car draped in a semi-fitted cover, which, I was informed, one of the family was to take ownership of. The walls were covered in signs, some enamel, some plaster and the more common tin type.

I was also informed that a local chap had made an offer for the collection of signs. They were keen to accept his offer, as they did not want a trickle of would be buyers visiting at all hours. It suited them to sell the whole collection to a single buyer. I asked why I had been called if a deal had already been done and was told that, although an offer had been made, they had not at this stage accepted. They had no idea of the value, but were sure the local guy was experienced in dealing with automobilia.

In this situation you realise quite quickly that this could have been a wasted journey, as perhaps you are only here to value, rather than buy. However, I was on my way south and the detour was not a great deal out of my way.

I immediately asked what the potential buyer had offered and the reply was that, as I was the so-called expert, it was my call to give a value.

I returned to the van and took out my notebook and pen and began inspecting and valuing each sign individually, at which point, I was informed that 'the other chap' took a very quick visual look and gave his price. Very interesting, I explained, but not my way. Twenty minutes later I totted up the figure for the 23 signs and wrote down the figure on a piece of paper, folded it in half and then told the son that I would give him my price once he had given me the other man's offer.

He paused a while, then said that he realised that I was a dealer and that I had to make a profit and, of course he expected my offer to be somewhat lower. At which point he told me the other offer and then proceeded to open the folded note. The expression on his face was a picture; my offer was almost double the offer the other guy had made.

"Is this your valuation, or a firm offer?" he asked. I told him that I would be happy to pay the amount written on the note for these signs and, what is more, I would be happy to take them here and now. I did ask if he wanted to consult his mother or, indeed, if he wished to telephone the other interested party, to see if he wanted to raise his offer. He replied that his mother was leaving it up to him and that he felt the other guy had put his hat into the ring but was, as he put it, trying it on.

I then wrote out a very detailed invoice/contract, which he signed, giving him the right to sell me the goods and a declaration that no other third party had claim over any of the items. This is a very important part in dealing with items that have belonged to a deceased person.

I have witnessed all to often families falling out over items when a person has passed away. Families that have been close for many years, ripped apart by jealousy and greed. Don't take the chance; cover yourself with the documents at point of sale. Of course, if the person signing does not have the official authority to sell, you could be victim of future problems. But, at least, you did everything at the point of sale to cover your back.

Remember dealers have to make a profit. We have to cover so many costs, wages, transport, property rents, insurance and so on. But a dealer also has a reputation to protect, and most dealers, including myself value their reputation above profit. So don't think for one minute that the guy in the pub, or the bloke you know at work will give you a better, or more honest offer. Remember the bloke from the pub is not interested in his dealing methods or his reputation; most are looking for a bargain at your expense.

AUTOMOBILIA ON QUEEN MARY 2

During the summer of 2014, I boarded the Queen Mary 2 at Southampton for a two-week voyage to Norway, taking in the Fjords and the North Cape. I was delighted to discover that Midge Ure, of Ultravox and Band Aid fame, was on board and would be giving several talks about his time in the music industry and his work with Band Aid.

A couple of days into the cruise I was having a conversation with the Entertainments Director regarding a form that I had been given by Cunard to complete. This would then enable me to register for their enrichment programme, and to give talks on board their ships. I explained that the form was still in my in-tray back at the office, and that I had been unable to complete it and make the journey down to Southampton for the clearance meeting due to workload.

At this point the director informed me that although I had not filled in the form, I could still give a talk on board as a guest speaker, and asked if I would be interested in doing this, to which I replied that I would give it some thought and let her know.

Most mornings on board ship, I find myself in the internet centre answering emails and trying to run my business at sea. With this in mind, I questioned whether or not I wanted to put myself under more pressure to deliver a speech on automobilia when, after all, this was my holiday and time to rest. So I came to the conclusion that although it would be quite an experience, if asked again I would have to decline.

During the next couple of days I found time to relax and to attend one of Midge Ure's talks, which was well presented, well supported and very interesting - and certainly a very hard act to follow for anyone else giving a talk.

People who have been on cruises will know that every night when you return to your stateroom, waiting for you is the ship's newspaper with the following days events and times listed. When my wife scanned through the paper she found that I was down to give a talk at 2pm the following day. At first I thought that she was pulling my leg. Looking for myself it was there in black and white: Talk on Automobilia by Robert Arnold at 2pm.

It was now 2am and in twelve hours time I was to make my début on board the Queen Mary 2. I awoke very early the following morning and began making notes in readiness for my talk. I went along to see the Entertainments Director to ask why I had not been informed and was told that she was in a meeting so I decided to head back to the internet suite to carry on with my preparation, as at this late stage, I was not about to let anyone down who was on board and looking forward to hearing me speak. So at 2pm that afternoon, two hundred miles inside the Arctic Circle, I began my talk.

I spoke about vintage pumps, signs and the early days of motoring. With a few snippets of my experience travelling around the UK, meeting some fascinating people and being shown some incredible collections.

One elderly lady had walked in with the aid of a stick and took her place at the rear of the room. I remember glancing over to her several times during the talk, thinking that she was there only because her dear husband would be interested in what I had to say. Several times I wondered if indeed she would rest her eyes and fall asleep. But, to my amazement, the longer I spoke the more interested she seemed to be.

Talks are scheduled for around forty-five minutes or so on sea days, so that passengers can flit from one activity to another and be governed by a time schedule. Aware of this, I glanced at my watch and on forty-five minutes I thanked all those who had attended and gingerly asked if anyone had any questions. Some twenty minutes later, and with no one yet leaving, including the elderly lady, I explained that I must finish so that everyone could go on to other events. A few people shook my hand and thanked me and, to my amazement, the elderly lady shook my hand and said how much she had enjoyed it, even though she had only come along to keep her husband company, and that it was one of her favourite talks she had attended on board cruise ships. At that point I must admit that a lump came into my throat.

Now, let's make this quite clear; Midge Ure at this point had given two talks and on both occasions it was standing room only, which must have given great satisfaction. But the response from this elderly lady had given me equal satisfaction, knowing that for over an hour this reluctant lady had enjoyed the world of automobilia.

Was this the first time that automobilia had been the topic of a talk on a Cunard ship, and would it be the last? Only time will tell.

FILM PROPS

For some time we have been supplying TV and film companies with props to use on film shoots. On one occasion a production company making a small budget film centred on a filling station, which was connected to the main film characters, contacted me. The props department were to build a mock filling station kiosk and we were asked to supply the petrol pump and several items to dress the scene. The film company agreed to hire the equipment and also to pay for me to stop in a hotel overnight near to the location, the idea being that it would be an early morning start with a full day of filming right through to a night shoot. They felt that it was important for me to be on set to advise on the workings of the items we had supplied, especially the petrol pump.

On the day prior to the shoot, the van was loaded and I set off for the location deep in the Welsh valleys. Late in the afternoon I arrived at the film location and found the kiosk on a disused road near the top of a Welsh mountain, with a security guard on site, drinking from a flask of tea. It was August but, by the feel of the wind and temperature, it could have been mistaken for December or January. It was this guys job to sit here and guard the site ready for filming the next morning. With no-one else around I decided to ring one of the production team to see if we could dress the scene now as opposed to a very early start the next day. He agreed and within an hour the set designer and crew members were on site to help me unload and position the props, as required. I then set off for my hotel for the overnight stay in the nearby village.

The next morning, with no pressure on me to arrive at the crack of dawn, I had a leisurely breakfast before returning to the location, where I found a crew of over thirty, caravans for the main actors, and cars and vans everywhere. Less than twenty-four hours prior to this, the scene was very different, with a solitary security guard with his flask and a petrol kiosk. Now the scene had been transformed into a full-blown film set, with people rushing about with headphones, walkie -talkies, mike booms, cameras and lighting equipment. Waterproof shelters had been erected to house monitors and equipment, which were being viewed by the producer, directors, assistant directors and technical staff. In another shelter, make-up and wardrobe were busily going about their work, transforming what I perceived as ugly ducklings into swans and indeed swans into ugly ducklings! It was a scene that can only be described as organised chaos and with, from what I could see, more emphasis on the chaos! But, no doubt, it would all come together. As I stood there in my automobilia coat, one of the crew came over and introduced herself as being the person that I had been dealing with. A few minutes later she left, only to return with the director and producer, who both shook my hand and expressed how pleased they were with the petrol pumps and items we had supplied. The director pointed out one of the crew, who was obviously the 'gofer' and said I should talk to him if I had any need for food and drink etc. during the day.

It was certainly a long day with several scenes to be filmed and one or two retakes, including a bizarre scene where one of the main actors was digging a grave and the crew were using smoke machines to set the scene. In fact one member of the crew, who had been instructed to climb a fence to dispense more smoke in the trees, actually fell over the fence and broke his ankle. Another bizarre situation occurred when a call went out on the walkie-talkie, to the man on the security gate over a mile away, to send the 'pet van' through onto the set. I was amazed to see the driver open the van and to appear with a canary in a cage. The canary was placed at the side of the grave and the next filming took place. I am still unaware of what role the canary played and at the time I was too uncomfortable to ask.

Filming went on throughout the day until just after 6 o'clock, when the director announced that the actors could now stand down and within a few minutes a couple of cars arrived to whisk them away. With this I enquired about the night scene, which I had been previously told that our items would be needed for, at which point one of the crew informed me that the day's filming had ceased and perhaps the night scene would be shot tomorrow. Hearing this I went to the director to enquire if this was indeed the case. He informed me that the night shoot would be taking place that evening with a skeleton crew and no actors, as this part of the film would have voice-overs and the participants in the film would be inside the building and could only be heard. We now had over a two-hour wait for the light to fade and darkness to fall before the night scenes could be worked on. The director and producer soon fled the site to a local hostelry, leaving just a skeleton crew and myself kicking our heels.

As the light faded and the director returned I was asked if I could remove the panel on the pump, so that the tech guys could install LED lighting. This was quickly done and very soon darkness had fallen over this cold and windy mountain spot. Cameras were at the ready, everyone in position and the tech guys switched on the lights in the pump. At which point the main camera person, being a petite French lady possibly in her late 20's, indicated with a "non, non, non." that she was obviously unhappy with the light reflecting on the glass of the pump. The tech boys shot onto the scene and made different variations of lighting before I stepped forward and offered the use of a torch which I had in the van. You can imagine the look I got from director, assistant director and tech boys as I uttered these words, until the camera lady suggested we give it a go. After returning from the van with the torch, I again removed the panel from the vintage pump, placed the torch into the position I felt would work best and secured the panel back onto the front of the pump. Cameras were then switched on again and the little French lady, to the annoyance I am sure of one or two around me, shouted "perfect, perfect."

In the next scene, standing by the director, I pointed out that at such a petrol station location, an exterior light would have been hanging for security at the premises when closed. He pointed out that they didn't have a light which was suitable, at which point I informed him that I had a lamp in the van which I thought would do the job. I supplied a second torch to light the said lamp, which was positioned and held in place by black tape. Again the camera lady uttered the words "perfect, perfect."

At around 11.30pm those three little words were uttered by the director to us all on this cold, windy and, by now, wet evening. "It's a wrap."

I quickly loaded the van, descended the mountain and was on my way home at just after midnight and, I must admit, on that journey home a smile came to my face more than once at the thought of me sitting in a cinema, watching a feature film with my wife, knowing that the scene in front of me involved two of my torches which had saved the day. How funny is the film business.

Some months later I received an invite from the film company to attend a BAFTA screening of the film in Cardiff and we did see the scene with the torches.

ALL THINGS AUTOMOBILIA

CAR FEST, GOODWOOD AND THE LONDON CLASSIC CAR SHOW

An events company in London, who were launching a new classic car show, to be held at the Excel Exhibition Centre in early 2015, contacted me in late Spring 2014. They approached me to ask if we could dress the scene at the press day launch of this new and exciting venture.

The press day was to take place in Knightsbridge, just around the corner from Harrods, at a venue set at the end of a mews. I delayed my decision until I had researched the company involved. On doing so I found them to be the people behind Chris Evan's Car Fest and the BBC Top Gear Live shows. I then quickly agreed to their request and, on the day of the press launch it was an early start to arrive in Knightsbridge just after 7.30am. The venue from the outside had the retro look of a 1940's/50's garage. One of our vintage petrol pumps was placed on either side of the doorway, with another three pumps situated inside the building. One pump inside stood at the side of a vintage Bentley, another at the side of an F1 car and the third was placed next to the Aston Martin DB, which was once owned by the Beatle Sir Paul McCartney. McCartney had purchased the car new in the 1960's and had a recording tape fitted in the vehicle, with Paul McCartney himself having confirmed that this was indeed where the first recording of Hey Jude had taken place.

On the outside of the building, the crew had built two twelve-foot backing boards, which we decorated with vintage signs. As the morning progressed, an array of super cars started to arrive, as well as members of the press and VIP guests. Although some of these cars were valued at over half a million pounds, on the day it was our vintage pumps that stole the show. One guy actually said that you could see Lamborghini's and Ferraris in London every day of the week, but he had never seen five such beautifully restored pumps together in one place.

The producer of Top Gear Live approached me and said how he thought our items, as he put it, brought the scene alive. At this point he asked me for one of our cards and proceeded to hand me one of his and told me that he would be in touch in the future. At that point I was unaware whom the gentleman was but obviously found out later when I read his card. It was at this press launch that I met so many important people and made so many influential contacts; Ed China and Mike Brewer from Wheeler Dealers and the TV Chef James Martin, who were all very complimentary of our items which were on show. I found James Martin to be a really nice guy, who is a true car enthusiast and we were to meet up again at the Classic Car Show itself, where we had a stand next to his restaurant.

Following the press launch, several leading companies contacted me with enquiries and interest in the hire of our pumps. In August of that year, I was on a cruise in Norway when contact was made to ask if I could supply vintage pumps for Chris Evans's Car Fest. I explained that I was away on holiday and would not be returning to the UK until Wednesday of the next week, which was some ten days away. They then went on to tell me that they did not need the pumps until the day after I got back, when they would have to be delivered to the site in Hampshire. For me this entailed driving up from Southampton on the Wednesday, loading the van on the same evening and travelling back down to Hampshire the following day. This was not something I was keen to do but when it was pointed out that we had an opportunity to have our pumps shown on the Friday night TV One Show, hosted by Chris Evans, I suppose the opportunity was too great to turn down. The pumps did indeed appear on the One Show on the Friday evening but, when Chris Evans cut to the presenter standing with my pumps, she held up a card, which unfortunately obstructed a sign with our name and number on - but at least our pumps had been on the TV.

Following the show, again we had an influx of enquiries. Some of which were of interest, but others which were dismissed. One interested party was Ford UK who wanted to hire one of our pumps for their stand at the Goodwood Revival. The theme for the stand was based around the Mustang, with the set displaying a fuel station on Route 66. We supplied a beautifully restored American pump, along with several other items. This venture again increased interest in our items and our website.

It was these events that were to spark the interest of several TV companies, with ideas looking at the world of automobilia. We have appeared on Porn Stars UK, Posh Pawnbrokers and Salvage Hunter starring Drew Pritchard. Because of time and, in some cases the format of the shows, we have declined many offers, but remain open to new ideas in the future.

INVEST AND ENJOY

Classic cars, vintage cars and automobilia whisk us back in time to memories of a golden age and thoughts of nostalgia. For those who are lucky enough to have an interest and the means to indulge in motoring nostalgia, they are fortunate that many items are seen as a good investment.

Unlike cars, vintage signs, pumps and globes are no longer produced. Cars that are being made at the moment will be seen in years to come as classics as times and models change. However, I can never see the petrol pumps that we use today on a daily basis, that are shaped more like an Ikea wardrobe, ever being deemed as collectable.

Over forty years ago I was offered a Rolls Royce Silver Cloud for three thousand pounds. It had belonged to a Knight of the Realm who, before he died, had lived in a Manor House a few miles from our village. I was contacted by a solicitor, who informed me that his client had written in his will that the car should be offered to me at half the market value, as a thank you and a gesture of the goodwill and kindness I had shown to him. Unfortunately, at the time, I could not raise the money to buy the vehicle and at the age of just over twenty years, I certainly did not have the means to run and maintain such a wonderful car and, of course, I passed the opportunity up. That same car today would, of course, be worth possibly in excess of forty thousand pounds. The strange thing is, many years later, I took in part exchange a mini van that at the time was immaculate. So much so that my wife used the van on many occasions to transport a carry-cot, pram and all the items associated with our first-born. The van at the time was worth around two hundred pounds; similar vehicles today are often seen for sale between fifteen thousand and twenty thousand pounds and a mint example for considerable more.

Some people's hobbies include golfing, fishing, football and cricket, all seen as excellent ways to spend your free time. But all pastimes cost money and although no doubt give endless hours of enjoyment, they give back little in the way of investment in the years that follow. Automobilia, classic and vintage cars, transport us back to a world of nostalgia, with most items being engineered and produced to a standard rarely seen in the manufacture of goods today. Whether you own a Ferrari, Lamborghini, Mini van, Ford Capri, vintage petrol pump, motoring signs or globes, the fact is if any of those items reside in your garage or man cave, there are few better feelings than to enter such a place on a dark winters night and sample the aroma of the nostalgic items before you. I have travelled around the country visiting some wonderful collections, some with Ferraris and some with only a run of the mill classic car or some with a modest collection of automobilia. But very often I will see, tucked in the corner, a chair that has seen better days and was once part of a three-piece suite used in the house. This gives the game away that this collector or enthusiast uses the space as a bolt-hole to enter and enjoy their world of nostalgia.

ACKNOWLEDGEMENTS

I would like to thank all those who have helped and encouraged me to write this book, especially Sara for her proof reading, Duncan for his help and advice regarding publication and my dear wife Jill for her hours of typing.

Thanks also to the characters and the many wonderful people who have supported my business over the years.

Thanks to you for buying this book. I do hope you enjoyed a glimpse into our world of automobilia.

We have another book planned for late 2016 which will include the full story of an amazing Ferrari collection on the south coast, some tales from my early garage days, my brief encounter with the world of motor racing, two ladies with a passion for Fiat 500s and Herbie the press car. Also the amazing tansformation of a concrete bunker into a wonderful collection of automobilia, in a stunning setting in the beautiful Cotswolds and an opening day, which included a turntable, an opera singer and a Ferrari. A story and a project that will never be repeated and was carried out by Automobilia-UK.

A percentage of the profits from the sale of this book will go to the Air Ambulance Appeal.

Please check out our website at automobilia-uk.com.

Email us at automobilia-uk@hotmail.co.uk

You can also find us on Facebook and Twitter.

Best wishes

Rob